The
SMALL and MIGHTY
Book of
Dinosaurs

Published in 2022 by OH!
An imprint of Welbeck Children's Limited, part of Welbeck Publishing Group.
Based in London and Sydney.

www.welbeckpublishing.com

Writer: Clive Gifford
Illustrator: Kirsti Davidson
Design and text by Raspberry Books Ltd
Editorial Manager: Joff Brown
Design Manager: Matt Drew
Production: Melanie Robertson

ISBN 978 1 83935 147 1

Printed in Heshan, China

10 9 8 7 6 5 4 3 2 1

FSC
www.fsc.org
MIX
Paper from
responsible sources
FSC® C020056

The
SMALL and MIGHTY
Book of
Dinosaurs

Clive Gifford and Kirsti Davidson

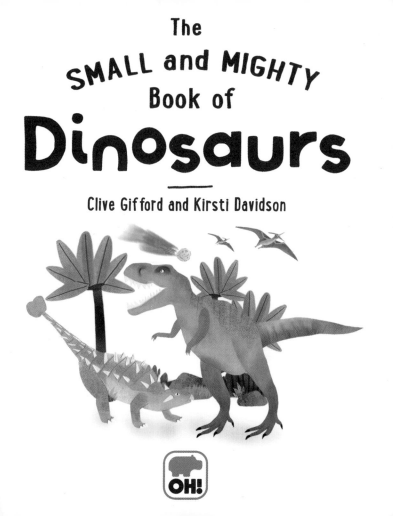

Contents

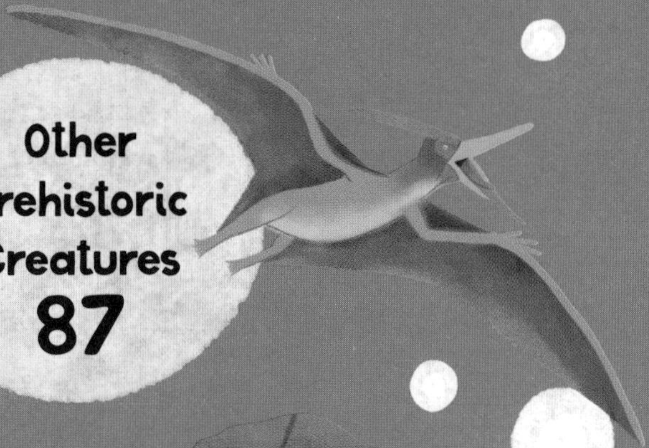

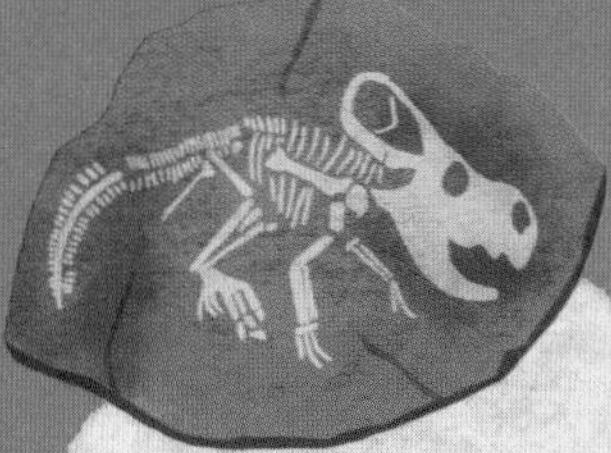

INTRODUCTION

～

Dinosaurs were reptiles—part of
a group of creatures that includes
crocodiles, tortoises, and lizards. They
dominated life on Earth for more than
140 million years. Although they died
out a long time ago, they astound and
fascinate people today with their size,
strangeness, and in some cases,
their fierceness.

In the past, people thought of all dinosaurs as large, slow-moving, scaly beasts. Science has shown that they were far more varied in size and shape than we first thought. Learning about dinosaurs is so exciting. There are still plenty of mysteries, and new discoveries are made every year.

Types
of
Dinosaurs

THE WORD "DINOSAUR" WAS
FIRST USED BY A BRITISH
NATURALIST NAMED
RICHARD OWEN IN 1842.
IT MEANS "FEARFULLY
GREAT LIZARD."

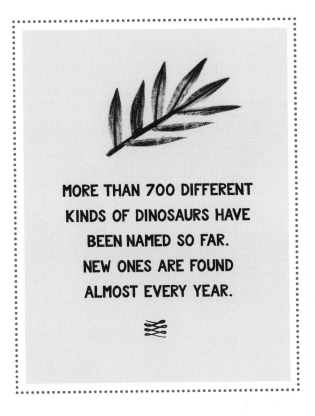

MORE THAN 700 DIFFERENT
KINDS OF DINOSAURS HAVE
BEEN NAMED SO FAR.
NEW ONES ARE FOUND
ALMOST EVERY YEAR.

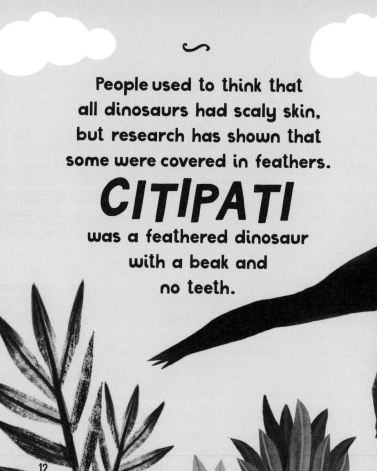

People used to think that
all dinosaurs had scaly skin,
but research has shown that
some were covered in feathers.

CITIPATI

was a feathered dinosaur
with a beak and
no teeth.

Citipati

Some dinosaurs were **really small**. *Parvicursor* weighed less than 10 oz., while *Epidexipteryx* weighed 6 oz.—less than the weight of an adult hamster.

STEGOSAURUS

was a dinosaur that grew to about 30 ft. long. These giants had large bony plates running along their backs, and spikes sticking out of their tails.

VELOCIRAPTOR

was nowhere near as big as it is sometimes shown in movies. In real life a *Velociraptor* was certainly fierce but only about the size of a turkey!

DINOSAURS DEVELOPED INTO TWO
LARGE GROUPS BASED ON THE
SHAPE AND POSITION OF
THEIR HIPS.

One group of dinosaurs,
the **BIRD-HIPPED**, had hips
similar to the hips of modern birds.
This group includes *Stegosaurus*
and *Triceratops*.

The other group was the
LIZARD-HIPPED
dinosaurs, which includes
Brachiosaurus and
Deinonychus.

Deinonychus lived around
110–120 million years ago. It was almost as tall as
a human and was equipped with deadly claws on both
hands and feet. **ONE VICIOUS CURVED CLAW**
on each foot measured 5 in. and could swivel
out of the way when the dinosaur
was running.

Dinosaurs appeared near
the beginning of the
MESOZOIC ERA—
a span of time which lasted from
245 TO 66 MILLION YEARS
ago—and died out at the end.
Dinosaurs had long gone by the
time people arrived, less than
half a million years ago.

The Mesozoic Era was split into three time periods, called the **TRIASSIC, JURASSIC,** and **CRETACEOUS**. Different dinosaurs existed within the different periods. A *Stegosaurus* would never have battled a *Tyrannosaurus rex*, for example: *Stegosaurus* lived in the Jurassic period, and *T. rex* lived more than **70 MILLION YEARS** later, in the Cretaceous period.

~

ALLOSAURUS

was a Jurassic meat eater that hunted
Stegosaurus. It stood up to 16 ft. tall.
Despite weighing several tons,
its powerful legs meant that it
could run fast—up to 20 mph.

The **JAWS** of an *Allosaurus* could open 2.5 ft. wide. In between it had two sets of **FEARSOMELY SHARP TEETH.**

CERATOPSIANS

were a group of plant-eating dinosaurs.
One of the **smallest** was tiny *Yinlong*
from China. It weighed only 30 lb., and
wouldn't reach the height of your knees.
So it was well-named—*Yinlong*
means "hidden dragon."

Many ceratopsians had **beaks like a parrot's** and large bony frills surrounding their heads. Many had horns on their heads for protection. Some walked on two legs, like *Yinlong*, while others walked on all fours.

Yinlong

TRICERATOPS

was bigger than a **minivan**. It could reach **30 ft.** long and weighed **6 tons**— more than a **monster** truck.

24

Kosmoceratops, a relative of *Triceratops*, **had 15 horns** sticking out of its head, including one protruding from each cheek.

HADROSAURS

were a large group of plant-eating dinosaurs with flattened jaws, a bit like the bill of a duck. One of the largest hadrosaurs we know about was *Shantungosaurus*, which grew up to 50 ft. long. That's more than twice the length of a large crocodile.

Maiasaura

All dinosaurs laid eggs.
A type of hadrosaur called
Maiasaura built nests of
earth before laying between
30 and 40 eggs.

SOME HADROSAURS COVERED THEIR EGGS WITH MOUNDS OF TWIGS AND LEAVES. AS THE PLANTS STARTED TO ROT AND DECAY, THEY GAVE OFF HEAT, WHICH WARMED THE EGGS. SMART!

MANY DINOSAUR BABIES GREW RAPIDLY AFTER HATCHING. SOME TYPES OF HADROSAURS DOUBLED IN SIZE IN JUST FOUR TO SIX WEEKS.

Before it was fully grown,
PARASAUROLOPHUS,
a type of hadrosaur,
walked on **TWO LEGS.**
As it grew up, it switched to
walking on all four legs.

Parasaurolophus had a strange bony crest on
top of its head with hollow tubes inside.
The crest could grow up to 6 ft. long.
Many dinosaur experts think it was used
to sound warnings or call out to other
members of the herd.

31

32

Dino Giants

SAUROPODS were the biggest of all DINOSAURS.

These giants of the prehistoric world stood on four incredibly stout legs that supported their great weight. Some sauropods may have grown more than 100 ft. long and weighed more than 50 tons.

To give an idea of the massive scale of these creatures, a single sauropod footprint, found in Australia in 2017, measured 5 ft. 9 in. long and almost 3 ft. wide! And a single thigh bone of a mystery sauropod was unearthed in France in 2019—it was taller than most people, measuring 6.5 ft.

AT AROUND 79 TO 85 FT.
LONG, *MAMENCHISAURUS*
WAS LONGER THAN
A TENNIS COURT!

MOST SAUROPODS HAD
SMALL, LIGHTWEIGHT
HEADS PERCHED ON LONG
NECKS. THIS ALLOWED THEM
TO STAND STILL IN ONE
PLACE YET REACH LOTS OF
DIFFERENT FOOD.

THE MOUTH OF *DIPLODOCUS* WAS FILLED WITH PEG-SHAPED TEETH. THESE WERE USED TO COMB TREE BRANCHES AND STRIP THEM OF THEIR LEAVES.

Diplodocus

Apatosaurus

38

Supersaurus

Many dinosaur experts think that
different types of sauropods
grazed together in the same areas.
Taller sauropods would have eaten higher
leaves, leaving lower-lying trees and plants
for shorter sauropods to feed on.

All
SAUROPODS
were vegetarian

and needed to eat plants all
the time to survive.

We think that *Apatosaurus* would
have eaten 880 lb. of food per day.
That's about the weight of
1,600 sandwiches.

SAUROPODS didn't chew their food—they just **swallowed it.** Some types swallowed stones, which stayed in the dinosaur's stomach and helped grind its food down. **These stones are known as gastroliths.**

DIPLODOCUS'S 23 ft. long neck was almost three times as long as a giraffe's.

SUPERSAURUS'S neck may have been even longer.

The neck of an adult **MAMENCHISAURUS** measured up to 50 ft. long—longer than a school bus.

EVERYTHING ABOUT THE
BIGGEST SAUROPODS WAS
SUPERSIZED.

TO PUMP BLOOD AROUND
ITS GIANT BODY,
A SAUROPOD'S HEART MAY
HAVE BEEN THE SIZE
OF A GARBAGE CAN AND
WEIGHED 440 LB.

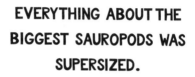

ACCORDING TO
THE AMERICAN MUSEUM
OF NATURAL HISTORY,
ARGENTINOSAURUS
MAY HAVE BEEN THE
HEAVIEST SAUROPOD OF ALL,
WEIGHING UP TO 90 TONS.

BRACHIOSAURUS
may have measured up to
100 FT. LONG.

With a strong and long neck, it held
its head high and may have been able
to reach tree leaves up to 40 ft.
above the ground.

Sauroposeidon,
another giant sauropod,
could stand 55 ft. high.
That's around three times
the height of a giraffe.

APATOSAURUS WASN'T QUITE AS TALL AS SOME OTHER SAUROPODS, BUT EXPERTS THINK IT COULD REAR UP ON ITS BACK LEGS TO REACH HIGHER FOOD SOURCES.

DESPITE BEING 70 FT. LONG AND WEIGHING AROUND 26 TONS, *APATOSAURUS* HAD A TINY BRAIN. SCIENTISTS HAVE WORKED OUT IT WEIGHED JUST 4 OZ.—LESS THAN ONE-TENTH OF THE WEIGHT OF A HUMAN BRAIN.

Some
SAUROPODS
were far smaller than
Argentinosaurus
and the other giants.
Magyarosaurus was a type of
dwarf sauropod that lived around
70 million years ago. It stood only
about as tall as an adult human
and weighed about a ton.

Argentinosaurus babies hatched from eggs a little smaller than a beach ball, so they must have grown incredibly fast to reach their adult length of over 100 ft.

Magnapaulia

THERE WERE OTHER PLANT-EATING
DINOSAURS THAT WERE NOT SAUROPODS
BUT STILL GREW TO BE MASSIVE.

MAGNAPAULIA WAS
A HADROSAUR THAT GREW
TO ABOUT 50 FT. LONG AND
WEIGHED 26 TONS.
AS MUCH AS THREE
T. REX DINOSAURS.

Hunters
and
Hunted

MANY DINOSAURS
WERE **PREDATORS**.
HUNTING OTHER
CREATURES.
THE FIRST DINOSAUR
TO BE NAMED (IN 1824)
WAS A TWO-LEGGED
HUNTER CALLED
MEGALOSAURUS.

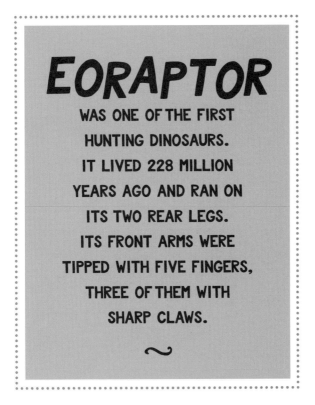

EORAPTOR

WAS ONE OF THE FIRST
HUNTING DINOSAURS.
IT LIVED 228 MILLION
YEARS AGO AND RAN ON
ITS TWO REAR LEGS.
ITS FRONT ARMS WERE
TIPPED WITH FIVE FINGERS,
THREE OF THEM WITH
SHARP CLAWS.

Smaller hunters like
VELOCIRAPTOR
may have hunted in packs,
taking turns to attack
a larger plant-eating
dinosaur and
wearing it out.

ENCOUNTERING A

UTAHRAPTOR

MUST HAVE BEEN TERRIFYING.
THIS 23 FT. LONG PREDATOR HAD
JAWS PACKED WITH TEETH, AND
SHARP CLAWS, INCLUDING
A 9 IN. CURVED CLAW ON
ITS TWO SECOND TOES.

Discovered in Canada, *Hesperonynchus* is one of the **SMALLEST** known dinosaurs that hunted and **ATE MEAT.** It was only about the size of a small chicken.

EVEN SMALLER WAS *ANCHIORNIS*, WHICH WAS DISCOVERED IN CHINA. THIS LIZARD-AND-INSECT-EATING DINOSAUR HAD FOUR WINGS, THE FRONT PAIR OF WHICH CONTAINED SHARP, SLENDER CLAWS. IT WAS ONLY 16 IN. LONG AND WEIGHED LESS THAN A CAN OF SODA.

The most famous
dinosaur hunter of all was
**TYRANNOSAURUS
REX.**

Its name means "king of the tyrant lizards." This fearsome meat eater grew to 40 ft. long and had eyes the size of tennis balls—good for spotting prey.

T. REX
had arms only 3 ft. long, so they were too short to reach its mouth.

DINOSAUR EXPERTS
THINK THAT, FAR FROM
BEING PUNY AND USELESS,
THIS DINOSAUR'S ARMS
WERE SHORT AND STRONG,
TIPPED WITH SHARP
CLAWS THAT COULD
SLASH AT PREY.

ACCORDING TO THE NATURAL
HISTORY MUSEUM IN BRITAIN,
A *TYRANNOSAURUS*
TYPICALLY WEIGHED
8 TONS—ABOUT AS MUCH AS
20 GRIZZLY BEARS.

THE **GIANT JAWS** OF A **T. REX**

could be 4 ft. long and were moved by extremely powerful jaw muscles. This gave it a bite at least three times as strong as a lion's—enough to crunch through bone.

Those jaws included 60 fearsome teeth. At the back were the bone-crunching teeth. Along the side were saw-edged teeth—some of them 8 in. long.

SPINOSAURUS
was one of the few hunting
dinosaurs even bigger than
T. rex. It measured 50 ft.
long—longer than a tractor
trailer—and weighed
up to 10 tons.

Spinosaurus was named for the spiny sail found on its back. Its long but slender snout probably meant that it mostly hunted and ate big fish, not other large dinosaurs.

Some plant-eating dinosaurs
were covered in
BONY ARMOR to
protect themselves from
ferocious attacks.

Ankylosaurus

ANYKLOSAURUS had a muscle-packed **TAIL** with a heavy, bony **CLUB** at its tip. Dinosaur experts think that when it was swung, it could have broken another dinosaur's bones, or at least given it a serious injury.

EUOPLOCEPHALUS even had armor on its eyelids!

ANKYLOSAURUS

used its armor to ward off attacks. It weighed 4-6 tons and only its belly was without armor. The rest of its body was covered in bony plates and ridges for defense. It could even fight off a *T. rex*.

73

Some ceratopsians, such as *Centrosaurus* and *Styracosaurus*, had **LARGE, BONY FRILLS** around their heads. This protected their necks from attacks by big hunters.

TRICERATOPS had a giant head, around 6 ft. long, with a bony frill plus three pointed horns for protection. The two horns above its eyes could each grow up to 3 ft. long.

Triceratops

Plant-eating

THERIZINOSAURUS

had a small, beak-shaped mouth, but it had protection from attack in the form of claws, the largest of which measured 2.5 ft. long.

THERIZINOSAURUS
means "scythe lizard"—
a strange name for a
strange-looking creature
with its large claws and
pot belly!

77

A row of sharp spines that looked
a bit like a big, spiky hairdo
stuck out of the long neck of
BAJADASAURUS.
The spines were nearly 24 in.
long and the dinosaur may have
used these for protection
against attack.

Other dinosaurs may have protected
themselves from hunters by roaming
the land in herds or, if they were
nimble, using their speed to
sprint away from danger.

STRUTHIOMIMUS

was one of the fastest dinosaurs.
It grew up to 14 ft. long and looked
a little like a giant ostrich. Experts
estimate it could reach speeds
of over 35 mph.

Running at high speed,
possibly to escape being eaten,
Struthiomimus would have taken
51 in. long strides, which is like
jumping past a sheep with every step!

One way to avoid being eaten was to be very big, like the SAUROPODS. But not all plant-eating dinosaurs were huge.

FRUITADENS

was about 28 in. long and the size of a pet cat. Its mouth featured both a beak and teeth for biting and chewing fruit and leaves.

NIGERSAURUS

was a sauropod with a wide, flat head and a mouth shaped like a mail slot. It had up to 500 teeth for cutting and chewing plants.

EDMONTOSAURUS

was another plant eater but with even more teeth than *Nigersaurus*. It is estimated that its mouth contained as many as 1,000 teeth, growing to replace one another as they wore out.

MANY DINOSAURS HAD **VERY SMALL BRAINS** FOR THEIR LARGE SIZE. THE MEAT-EATING

TROODON

WAS 8 FT. LONG, MAKING IT A RELATIVELY SMALL DINOSAUR. ITS BRAIN, THOUGH, WAS LARGE COMPARED TO OTHERS— IT WAS ABOUT THE SIZE OF A SMALL ORANGE.

Troodon had eyes that were larger than average for its size. They were about 2 in. wide. Big eyes allowed it to spot small prey such as lizards and small mammals. Its eyes also faced forward, to help it focus on prey while hunting.

Other Prehistoric Creatures

DINOSAURS WERE REPTILES THAT
LIVED ON LAND. THEY SHARED THEIR
SURROUNDINGS WITH OTHER
EXTRAORDINARY CREATURES
ON LAND. MANY DIFFERENT PREHISTORIC
CREATURES LIVED IN THE SEA OR
FLEW THROUGH THE AIR.

ICHTHYOSAURS

WERE COMMON HUNTING SEA REPTILES
THAT LOOKED A LITTLE LIKE SUPERSIZED
DOLPHINS. AN AMAZING ICHTHYOSAUR FOSSIL
FOUND IN CHINA IN 2010 CONTAINED
ANOTHER BIG REPTILE, A 13 FT. LONG
THALATTOSAUR, SWALLOWED
WHOLE IN ITS STOMACH.

OPHTHALMOSAURUS

was an ichthyosaur whose eyes
were about 9 in. in diameter—
almost as big as a dinner plate.
It used its enormous eyes to help
it hunt in the gloom of deep seas.

The largest known
ICHTHYOSAUR
was *Shastasaurus*. It reached
a length of **70 FT.**
—about twice the length
of a school bus.

LIOPLEURODON
had a long snout full of
teeth, some over
10 IN. LONG.
Scientists think it
feasted on large fish,
squid, and other
sea creatures.

KRONOSAURUS

was similar to *Liopleurodon* but, at **30-36 ft. long,** a little larger. A quarter of its length was made up by its huge skull, containing teeth the size of a **12 in. ruler.**

ELASMOSAURUS

had a neck about 20 ft. long—longer than a giraffe is tall. It was made up of 70 neck bones—10 times the number found in a human neck.

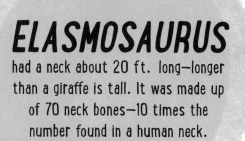

Elasmosaurus was a plesiosaur— one of a group of sea reptiles with long necks and small heads. Another plesiosuar, *Albertonectes*, had an even longer neck. It contained 76 bones and measured over 23 ft.

PTEROSAURS
were flying reptiles and were the first creatures, after insects, to fly (rather than just glide).

There are more than
130 KNOWN SPECIES of pterosaurs.
New ones get discovered all the time. In
2019, a large pterosaur from Canada
was named *Cryodrakon*, meaning
"frozen dragon."

DIMORPHODON

was one of the first flying reptiles. Scientists think it first existed around 200 million years ago and had a wingspan of 5 ft.

Dimorphodon flapped its thick wings and probably used its long, stiff tail to keep it balanced as it flew.

Many **pterosaurs** had clawed hands positioned on the front edge of their wings.

The biggest pterosaur
of all was called
QUETZALCOATLUS.
Its wings measured
36 ft. from tip
to tip.

WHEN ON
THE GROUND,
QUETZALCOATLUS
WOULD HAVE STOOD
TALLER THAN
A GIRAFFE!

PTEROSAURS HATCHED FROM
SOFT-SHELLED EGGS WITH
THEIR WINGS FULLY FORMED.
THIS MEANS THEY COULD
PROBABLY FLY SHORTLY
AFTER HATCHING.

Nemicolopterus

One of the smallest
pterosaurs was
Nemicolopterus,
with a wingspan of
just 8–10 in.

PTERANODON

belonged to a group of flying reptiles.
Some had giant wingspans of 23 ft.
These wings were too big to
flap for long, so experts think
these reptiles mostly soared
like a glider plane.

Unlike many
prehistoric creatures, *Pteranodon*
had no teeth. Instead, it used its
long, slender beak to scoop up fish
swimming near the surface
and swallowed them whole.

The flying reptile

PTERODACTYLUS

walked on all fours when on the ground.
Scientists think it folded up its
wings a little like an umbrella
when moving or resting on land.

Pterodactylus

had a long beak filled with
90 sharp, cone-shaped teeth.

Ctenochasma

had even more—as
many as **400**.

PTEROSAURS
AND DINOSAURS EXISTED
ALONGSIDE MANY OTHER TYPES
OF ANIMALS. *MEGAXANTHO* WAS
A **GIANT CRAB** WHICH
HAD A MOVABLE FINGER
ON ITS GIANT RIGHT CLAW
THAT COULD CRUSH THE HARD
SHELLS OF SHELLFISH.

The world's
BIGGEST KNOWN SNAKE
lived in South America shortly after
the dinosaurs died out.
TITANOBOA
grew to lengths of 42 ft.
and was estimated to
weigh a ton.

BEELZEBUFO

was a giant prehistoric frog
about the size of a beach ball.
Scientists estimate that it could
have bitten into baby dinosaurs
with the same force as
a tiger's jaws.

The world's largest bony fish lived around 165 million years ago. *LEEDSICHTHYS* grew at least 54 ft. long. It may have weighed as much as 50 tons—about the weight of eight African elephants.

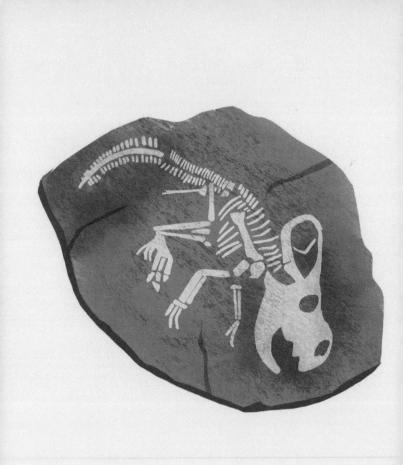

How We Know About Dinosaurs

Much of what we know about
dinosaurs comes from the
FOSSILS they left behind.
Fossils are the preserved
remains, or traces,
of once living things.
They are usually found
in rocks.

PALEONTOLOGY

is the science of studying prehistoric life.
Some paleontologists seek out new
fossils buried in rock. Others work
like detectives, piecing fossils together
like a jigsaw puzzle and using computers
and microscopes in the hunt for
other clues about how dinosaurs
looked and lived.

DINOSAUR FOSSILS
HAVE BEEN FOUND ON
EVERY CONTINENT
AROUND THE WORLD,
INCLUDING ANTARCTICA.

Cryolophosaurus lived in Antarctica around 190 million years ago and was one of the first two-legged meat-eating dinosaurs to be discovered there.

At that time, Antarctica had a much warmer climate than today. Also, it was not as far south as it is now!

THE ROYAL TYRREL MUSEUM

in Canada has an incredible collection of more than 160,000 fossils.

More than a thousand dinosaurs and tens of thousands of other fossils are housed in China's **Shandong Tianyu Museum of Nature.**

Xu Xing from China has discovered or named more new dinosaurs than any other living paleontologist— over 55 and still counting.

Among his
many discoveries was
SINOSAUROPTERYX—
an amazing winged
dinosaur covered
in feathers.

THE BONE WARS

was a fierce rivalry in the 1800s between two American fossil hunters, **Othniel Marsh** (who discovered *Stegosaurus* and *Diplodocus*) and **Edward Drinker Cope** (the first to describe *Elasmosaurus* and *Coelophysis*).

Cope

Cope and Marsh started out as friends but began fighting over new areas to dig for fossils. To try to outdo one another, they both paid people to fossil hunt for them and ship fossil bones to them to study. Their rivalry sparked the discovery of dozens of new dinosaur species, including *Triceratops* and *Allosaurus*.

Marsh

IN GENERAL, ONLY THE HARD PARTS OF DINOSAURS, SUCH AS **BONES** AND **TEETH**, SURVIVE AS **FOSSILS**. USUALLY, PARTIAL **SKELETONS** ARE FOUND WITH SOME BONES MISSING.

PALEONTOLOGISTS HAVE TO INVESTIGATE AND ESTIMATE HOW THE REST OF THE DINOSAUR MIGHT HAVE LOOKED.

Mistakes have sometimes been made, especially in the early days of paleontology in the 1800s. When

IGUANODON

fossil skeletons were first discovered, they were reassembled with a **SPIKY HORN FOR A NOSE.** Later experts realized the spikes actually belonged on the tips of the dinosaur's thumbs.

126

In **1971**, two fossilized dinosaurs—

a *PROTOCERATOPS*
and a *VELOCIRAPTOR*

—were found locked in combat in a desert in Mongolia.
The discovery, by a group of Polish fossil hunters
that included Teresa Maryańska, is thought of as
one of the most spectacular fossil finds of all time.

DINOSAUR FOOTPRINTS HAVE BEEN FOUND PRESERVED IN ROCK ALL OVER THE WORLD. A ROW OF THESE, CALLED A TRACKWAY, GIVES DINOSAUR EXPERTS CLUES AS TO HOW THE CREATURE MOVED AND HOW QUICKLY.

In 2009, a 500 ft. long trackway of dinosaur footprints was discovered in a French village. They were made about 150 million years ago by a giant sauropod dinosaur that was 100-115 ft. long.

In 1811, 12-year-old

MARY ANNING

(along with her brother)
discovered the first complete fossil
of an ichthyosaur in the cliffs of
Lyme Regis in southern England.

Mary found many more fossils,
including the first plesiosaur in
1823 and one of the first examples
of a pterosaur five years later.

Mary Anning was
not the only

CHILD
FOSSIL HUNTER.

In 1993, 14-year-old Wes Linster
discovered a fossil of an
unknown species of dinosaur,
later named *Bambiraptor*,
in Glacier National Park, Montana.
In 2020, 12-year-old Nathan
Hrushkin discovered a
HADROSAUR FOSSIL in the
Badlands of Alberta, Canada.

Three
DIPLODOCUS

fossil skeletons were discovered
in 2008. They were named Apollonia,
Prince, and Twinky and later sold
to a museum in Singapore
for **$5.8 million.**

THE FIRST *T. REX* SKELETON
WAS DISCOVERED IN HELL CREEK,
MONTANA, IN 1902 BY FAMOUS
AMERICAN FOSSIL HUNTER
BARNUM BROWN.

IN 1983, AN AMATEUR
FOSSIL HUNTER, WILLIAM
WALKER, DISCOVERED THE
FIRST KNOWN CLAW OF A

BARYONYX

DINOSAUR IN A CLAY PIT IN SURREY,
ENGLAND. HE WENT ON TO DIG OUT
A FULL FOSSIL SKELETON, REVEALING
BARYONYX AS A FEARSOME TWO-LEGGED
PREDATOR MORE THAN 23 FT. LONG.

Southern Argentina has proved a rich source of fossils. *Herrerasaurus* was named after a goat herder from Argentina named Victorino Herrera. In 1959, he was the first to find fossils of this type of dinosaur.

Troodon fossils have been found inside the chilly Arctic Circle. This makes it probably the most **NORTHERLY DINOSAUR** of all.

Fossilized dinosaur poop is called

COPROLITE.

It can tell dinosaur experts a lot
about what the creatures ate.

American George Frandsen is
a coprolite collector. He has
entered Guinness World Records
with his collection of
1,277 pieces of dinosaur poop!

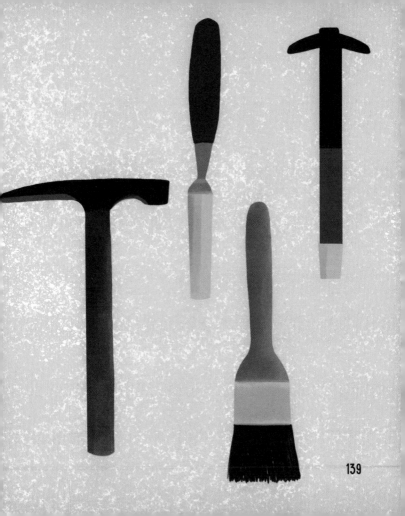

In 2020, a *T. rex* fossil skeleton named Stan became the world's most expensive dinosaur. Stan was sold at auction for a record **$31.8 million**. The second-most-expensive dinosaur was another *T. rex*, Sue, who was sold in 1998 for over **$8.3 million**.

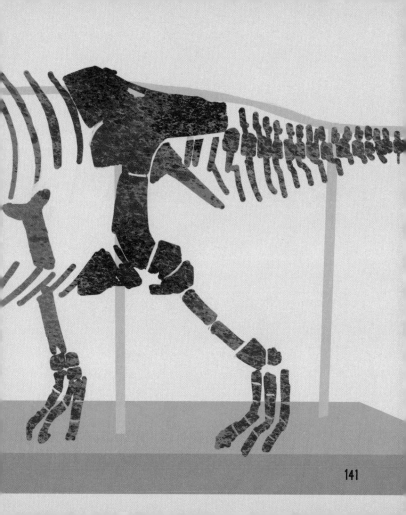

141

NO ONE IS COMPLETELY CERTAIN
HOW DINOSAURS DIED OUT SUDDENLY
66 MILLION YEARS AGO.
THE MOST ACCEPTED THEORY IS THAT
A LARGE ASTEROID FROM SPACE
CRASHED INTO EARTH.
ITS IMPACT FILLED THE
**ATMOSPHERE WITH
DUST,** WHICH BLOCKED OUT
A LOT OF SUNLIGHT AND COOLED
THE PLANET'S CLIMATE.

VOLCANOES

MAY HAVE ALSO CONTRIBUTED TO DINOSAURS DYING OUT. MANY MAY HAVE LEAKED LARGE AMOUNTS OF **POISONOUS GASES** INTO THE ATMOSPHERE AND HELPED CHANGE THE CLIMATE.

SOME CREATURES
SURVIVED, INCLUDING TURTLES,
SHARKS, AND EARLY BIRDS,
WHICH ARE THE DESCENDANTS OF
LIZARD-HIPPED DINOSAURS.

MANY NEW ANIMALS DEVELOPED
AFTERWARD, INCLUDING
MONKEYS, CATS . . .
AND US!